Painting On Glass

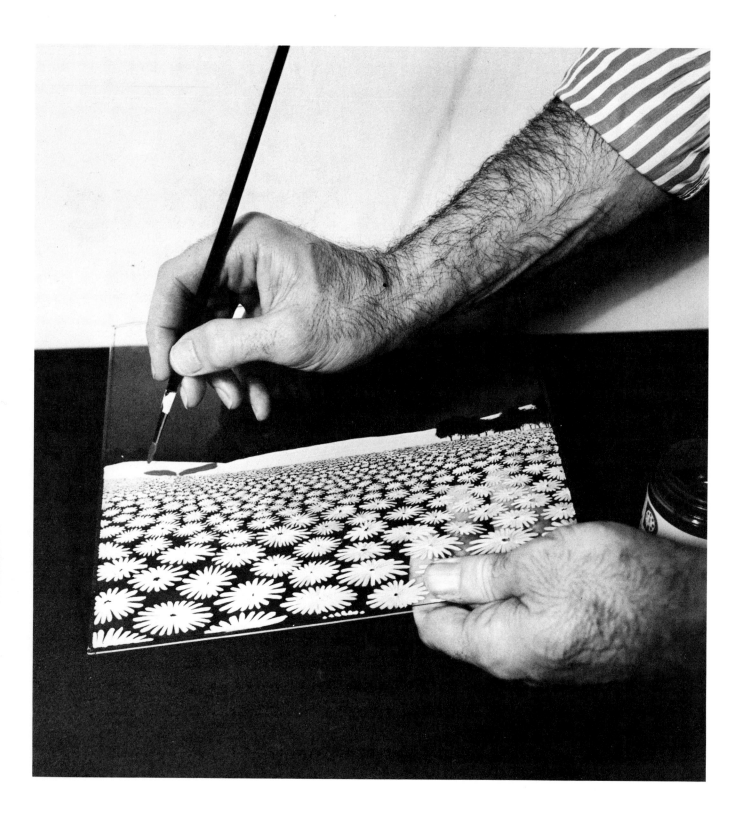

Painting
On
Glass

Jack Kramer

 VAN NOSTRAND REINHOLD COMPANY
New York Cincinnati Toronto London Melbourne

Printed in the United States of America
Photographs by Matthew Barr
Drawings by Michael Valdez
Finished glass paintings (shown in color) by Robert Johnson
Designed by Loudan Enterprises

Published in 1977 by Van Nostrand Reinhold Company
A division of Litton Educational Publishing, Inc
450 West 33rd Street, New York, NY 10001, U.S.A.

Van Nostrand Reinhold Limited
1410 Birchmount Road, Scarborough, Ontario M1P 2E7, Canada

Van Nostrand Reinhold Australia Pty. Limited
17 Queen Street, Mitcham, Victoria 3132, Australia

Van Nostrand Reinhold Company Limited
Molly Millars Lane, Wokingham, Berkshire, England

16 15 14 13 12 11 10 9 8 7 6 5 4 3 2 1

Library of Congress Cataloging in Publication Data

Kramer, Jack, 1927–
    Painting on glass.

    Includes Index.
    1. Glass-painting and staining. I. Title.
TT298.K72   748.5   77-77971
ISBN 0-442-20821-9

Contents

AUTHOR'S NOTE

In the 1950s I was a representative for a decorative-glass manufacturing company in Chicago. This company painted colored designs on glass, which was then used both fired and unfired for stove panels, signs, and other uses. As a representative I roamed the factory and became acquainted with the process of painting on glass. The factory silk-screened most of the decorations, but the prototypes were hand-painted. I spent many hours watching employees paint on glass, and much of the material for this book was actually gathered then.

I want to offer my appreciation to the Hamilton Glass Company and to Beeco Associates of Illinois, with a special thanks to Cliff Wolper. I also want to thank several craftsmen in the California area who shared their knowledge of more recent glass-painting techniques with me. And my thanks to Richard Becker, for his research on the history of glass painting; to Matthew Barr, for his photographs; to Michael Valdez, for his drawings; and to Robert Johnson, for his paintings on glass, which are reproduced here in full color.

Introduction:
History of Glass Painting

To transform a clear sheet of glass into a work of art is magic, because glass is so responsive to color. Painting the surface of glass with a variety of media can create myriads of pictures. The ancient Egyptians painted glass with gold, and since the twelfth century artisans of all countries have used enamel on glass. Enamel-painted goblets were especially popular in seventeenth-century Germany. The enamels were usually baked on after the initial painting, but some goblets were enameled by the cold-color process, which is still used in the manufacture of decorative stove panels.

Old church windows are perhaps the most striking example of painting on glass. The painting was first executed in a dark brown, and then the window was fired to permanently adhere the paint to the glass. Craftsmen eventually found that, by adding a silver oxide to the glass, they could obtain a beautiful amber color. This method of glass painting was called *Schwarzlot.*

The history of glass painting extends well back into antiquity, but the art was most popular between 1740 and 1880. Ancient bottles and cups were painted in cold colors (not fired): gold leaf was adhered to the surface. True reverse paintings on glass probably originated in Italy between 1265 and 1270, and by the late Renaissance glass paintings, usually taken from works of famous artists of the time, were commonly used in churches. In the baroque and rococo periods this type of painting was refined, and eventually the painting process was applied to mirrors, particularly in late 17th-century France and England.

The demand for glass paintings was so heavy that urban production could not keep up with it, and craftsmen in rural areas started a true folk art. By 1800 both professional glassmakers and rural peasants were engaged in the production of glass paintings. The popularity of glass paintings is documented by the fact that in a single glassworks in Bavaria 380,000 paintings were made in one decade (around 1860). The trend continued until the end of the 1800s when wars caused the decline of glass painting and the advent of colored lithographs.

The history of painting on glass is indeed rich. The craft was practiced in Spain, Italy, Turkey, Syria, Persia, France, England, India, China, and America. It is thus not a new phenomenon but rather some new techniques applied to a very old and exciting art and craft.

1. Glass Know-how

Glass is an age-old material that has been used in various ways throughout history. Today it is used primarily for windows in buildings and for industrial products such as oven doors and other household appliances. It is even used in pinball machines. But glass can also be used in a decorative way: vases, bowls, plates, and the stained-glass windows of yesterday (so popular today) are still other ways in which glass contributes to our daily life.

Decorating clear glass with paint can create many different types of useful accent pieces that will add beauty to the home: windows, plaques, pictures, and so forth. There are indeed many, many ways to decorate glass—engraving and etching, for example—but this book deals mainly with painting. With your imagination and the right know-how there are many avenues to follow. This book shows and tells you how to get the most out of paint and glass (both relatively inexpensive) and to create a myriad of handsome objects for indoor use.

You will work mainly with clear or mirrored flat glass (sheets of glass) that is painted on the front or back surface and left unfired. This means that the paint is not baked in and is thus susceptible to scratching or mishandling. With ordinary usage, however, decorative items will last several years. Most commercially painted glass products—oven doors, for example—are fired at high heat to make the color permanent.

The projects in this book include windowpanes, wall hangings, plaques, easel pictures, folding pictures, and other decorative items, all made without expensive equipment. Only paint and brushes are needed. Almost anyone can make these projects with some knowledge of glass and paints. Glass painting, a combination of art and craft, will open new doors to the world of do-it-yourself—enter!

FLAT GLASS

Flat glass, like lumber, comes in various thicknesses and grades. Very thin glass is $\frac{1}{64}''$ thick; very thick glass is 1" thick. Window glass, which is usually $\frac{1}{16}''$ or $\frac{1}{8}''$ thick and which you will mainly be working with, is available in two grades: A, which has little or no flaws, and B (commercial glass), which contains some small marks or seeds but none exceeding $\frac{1}{32}''$ in length.

Standard window glass, or B glass, is an imperfect product with inherent flaws. B glass is rolled; that is, it is poured in a liquid state and put through rollers to achieve thickness and flatness. SSA or SSB ($\frac{1}{16}''$ thick) and DSA and DSB ($\frac{1}{8}''$ thick) window glass has some waves, since it has gone through a roller process.

Window glass comes in boxes of 50 or 100 square feet and in sizes of 8" × 10" to 36" × 60". Glass is priced by the even inch; since you do not need too many sheets, buy by the piece by the even inch rather than by a specific size. If you buy by size, you can pay more: for example, if you want an 8⅛"-×-10¼" size, you will have to pay for the 10"-×-12" size and have it cut.

The glass that you buy usually has clean-cut edges, which means that the edges will be sharp. Always specify seamed or ground edges, which means that the sharp edges have been removed. (To cut your own glass, see the last section of this chapter.)

Sheet Glass

Sheet glass is crystal glass, which means that it is $\frac{3}{16}''$ or $\frac{7}{32}''$ thick. Heavier (thicker) glass is stronger, which is what you want for some decorated panels. Sheet glass costs more than window glass, but its added thickness gives it brilliance and luminescence when it is painted.

Small pieces of crystal glass—say, 10" × 20"—are relatively inexpensive and, like window glass, should be bought by the even inch for economy. Ground or seamed edges should also be specified. Sheet glass is also a rolled glass.

PLATE GLASS AND PATTERNED GLASS

Plate glass is polished on both surfaces by huge buffer wheels in order to eliminate all waviness. It is 25 percent more costly than window and sheet glass but is perfect if you want a very fine product. Polished plate glass is available in $\frac{1}{8}''$ and $\frac{1}{4}''$ thicknesses. Order plate glass by the even inch, with all edges seamed or ground.

Although clear glass is used for most of the projects in this book, patterned flat glass can be used in glass painting. In fact, the pattern itself can often be incorporated into the design.

STAINED GLASS

Stained glass, also called cathedral glass, antique glass, or flashed glass, is transparent colored glass. It can have ripples or mounds on one surface, with the other surface smooth; both surfaces textured; or both surfaces smooth (although the last type is hard to find).

The most popular color is amber; amber stained glass can be used as a painting surface. Pale blue is another stained-glass color that lends itself to painting. You can also use colored sheets—ruby, blue, amber—and cut them into small pieces. Make a pattern from the small pieces and then glue the pieces onto clear glass for a dramatic effect. This stained-glass-on-clear-glass method is discussed in Chapter 6.

Stained glass is slightly thicker ($\frac{3}{16}''$) than standard SSB window glass but is cut in the same manner. It costs twice as much as clear glass and is sold at glass stores and craft shops.

CUTTING GLASS

Cutting glass is easy with a small, inexpensive cutting wheel set into one end of a metal-handled glass cutter. The idea behind glass cutting is to score or fracture the glass *only* when you make the cut. The fracture causes the molecules to separate along the scored line. You must break the glass immediately before the separated molecules heal themselves. The secret of using the glass cutter (available at hardware stores) is to apply the pressure with neither too heavy nor too light a touch.

To actually break the glass, place a long pencil or strip of wood underneath the score line. Press down on the glass with the palms of your hands, one palm on each side of the cut, with just the right amount of pressure. The impact separates the glass cleanly.

To cut glass, first be sure that it is clean. Wipe it with turpentine, wash it with detergent, rinse it in warm water, and dry it thoroughly. After the glass is clean, set the pane on a level table covered with an old carpet or bath towel. Hold the cutter almost perpendicular and dip the cutting wheel into oil. To make a straight cut, place the cutter about 1/32" from the edge of the glass (to avoid edge chipping) and make a firm and continuous cut without lifting the cutter. You will know that you are doing it properly if the cutter makes a smooth and even noise. As soon as the glass is scored, place the wooden pencil directly under the score line and immediately press your palms on each side of the line. Apply pressure, and the glass will separate. If the glass does not separate, tap gently along the scored line with the end of the cutter; a fracture should develop along the line. Apply equal pressure to the two sides of the fracture line and snap the glass apart.

Cutting shaped pieces of glass—curves, arcs—requires more expertise. For these cuts you will need cardboard patterns. Place the patterns on the glass and score around them. To separate a thin glass strip from a wider piece, use a glass pliers with the grasping edges covered with tape. Grasp the narrow side of the glass with the pliers and the other side with your hands; snap off the small piece with the pliers. Corners or slight projections can be nipped off with the indented part of the glass cutter or with flat-nosed pliers.

No matter what kind of glass you are using or what kind of cut you are making, you should follow certain safety precautions. Sharp edges will cut you, so wear an old pair of household gloves. Do not grasp or hold glass by its edges, or you will be cut. Always keep your body and feet at a safe distance from the cutting table and never cut glass at close range—that is, close to your face. If you are reasonably careful, you will have no accidents.

Thin glass (1/16" or 1/8" thick) is easier to cut than thick glass. Cut glass 3/16" or 1/4" thick only after you have gained experience in cutting thinner glass. And if the idea of cutting glass frightens you altogether, buy precut glass (but remember that it is more expensive than buying panes and cutting pieces yourself).

To store glass, set it on edge. An excellent way to store small glass panes is to set them on a carpeted floor against a wall at a safe angle and to slip-sheet them with paper.

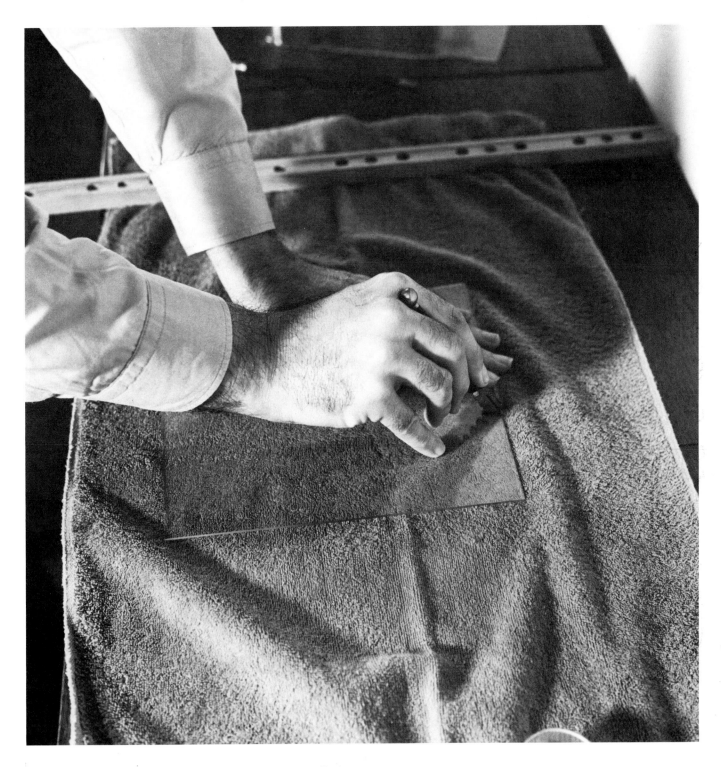

1. To score glass, hold the glass cutter almost perpendicular and make a cutting line with a straightedge ruler or a piece of wood.

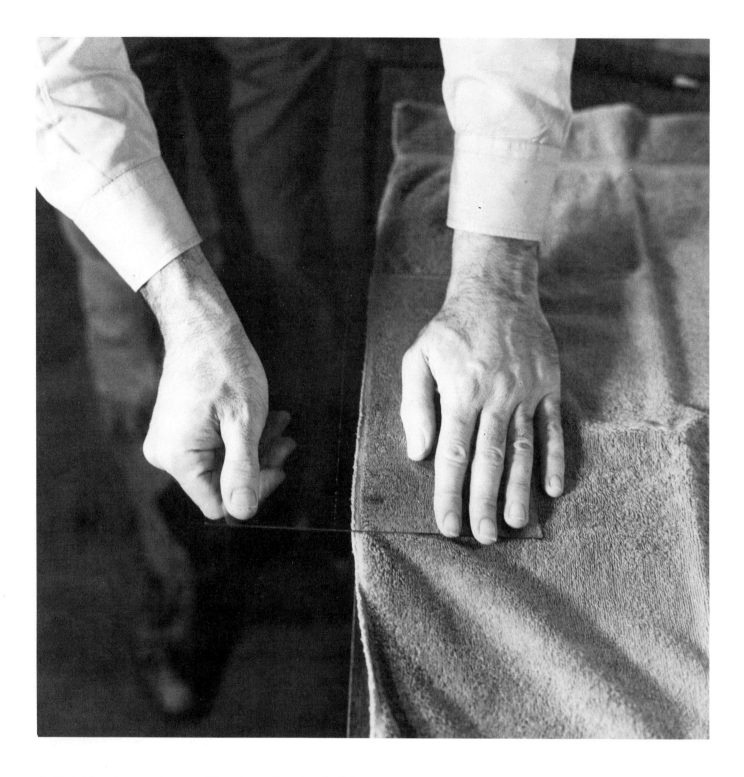

2. To cut the glass, set the scored line 1″ over the edge of a flat surface such as a table covered with a towel or carpet. Snap the glass down and out.

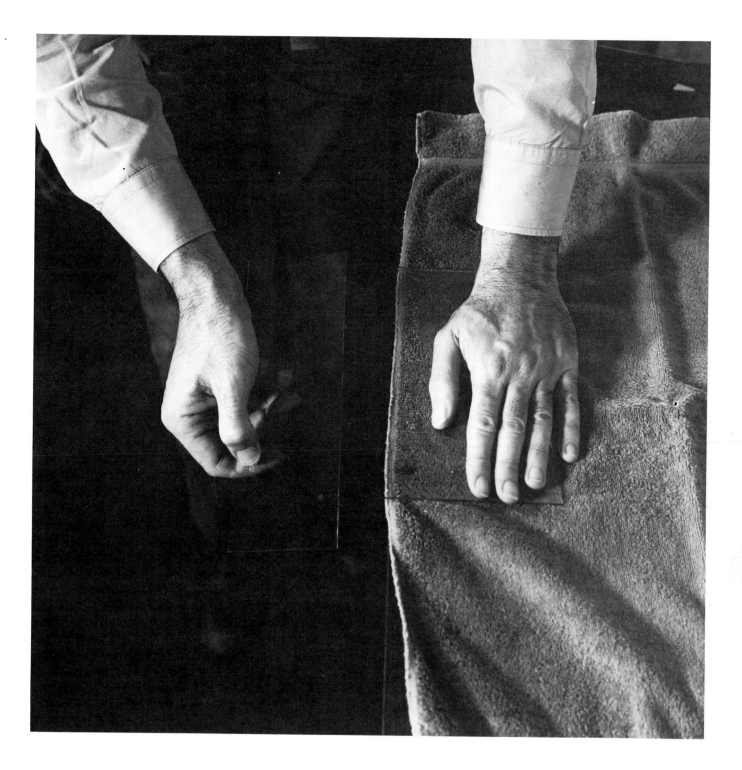

3. Break the glass with a slight flex of the wrist.

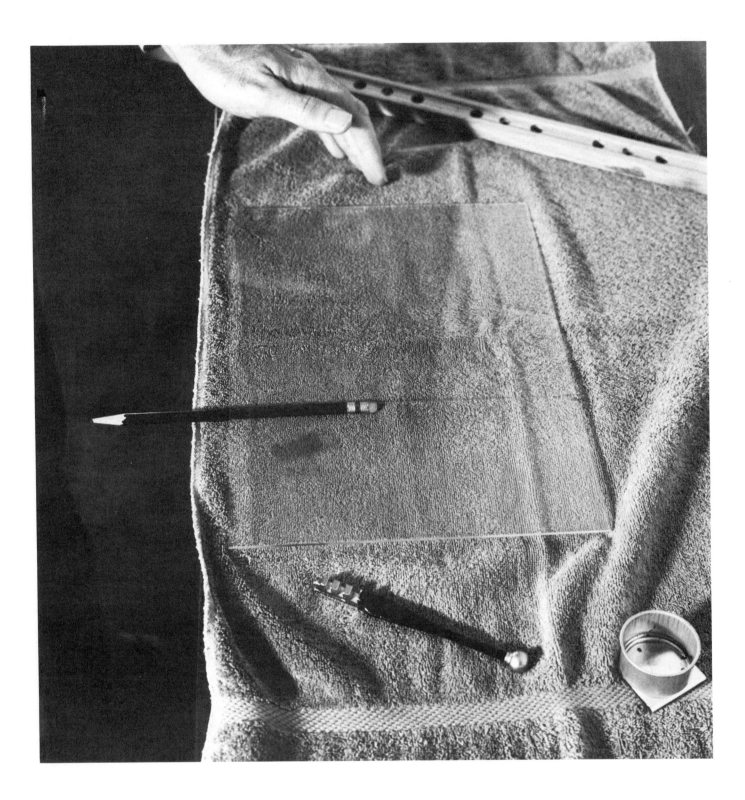

4. Another way to cut the score line is to immediately insert a
pencil under it and to press down firmly with your palms, one hand
on each section of the glass. The glass should separate easily.

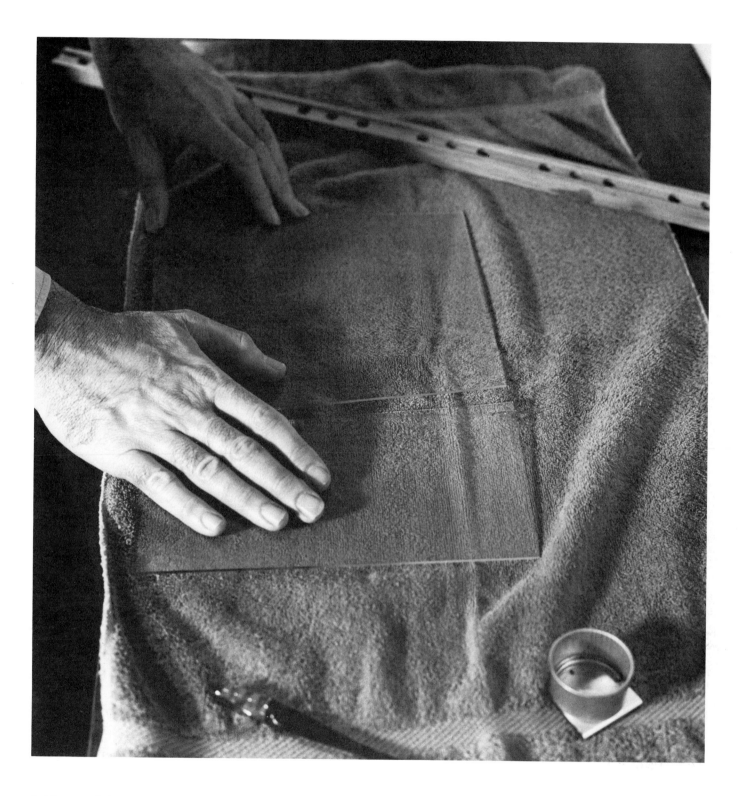

5. Glass, ready to use.

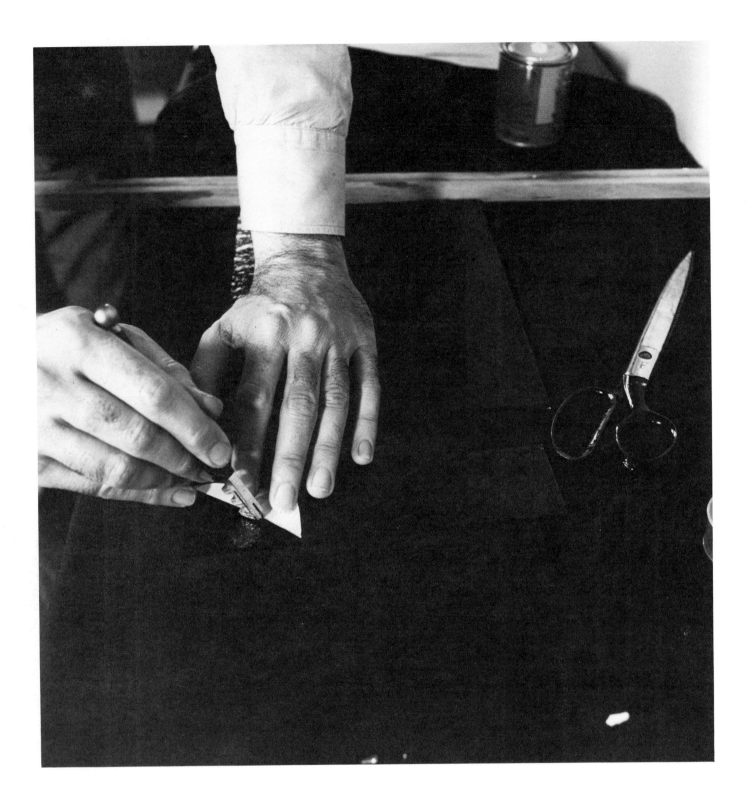

6. To cut small pieces of glass, use a cardboard pattern and make clean score lines.

7. Put a pencil under the score line to separate it from the pane or, with pliers (the tip wrapped in masking tape), grasp the scored piece and pull gently.

2. Getting Started

For any hobby or project a suitable place to work is half the battle (proper equipment is the other half). Glass painting requires only a level table. Cover the table with white vinyl or wrapping paper for better visibility and protection: you will be using paints, turpentine, and wet brushes, and some spilling, even if you are experienced, will occur.

Be sure that the area you are working in is well lighted. This is especially important for glass painting because glass is reflective: you want to be able to see exactly what you are doing, especially if you are painting fine lines.

EQUIPMENT AND MATERIALS

Use good-quality sable brushes (sold at art stores). These brushes are expensive, but with proper care they last a long time. Sable brushes are very fine, soft, and flexible, and they come in many different thicknesses. For most glass painting you need brushes with fine points. You will need #0 and #1 brushes for painting pattern lines and #3 or #4 brushes (broad points) for filling in areas. You will also need several brushes of each type if you are using many colors.

When you finish using a brush, wipe all excess paint from it with paper towels or a cloth; dip the brush into paint thinner or turpentine and "paint" on newspaper to remove the paint from the brush. Wash the brush with mild soap and warm water and rinse thoroughly. Protect your brushes: if you do, they will last for years.

To mix colors and to spread out paint, you will need a palette, which can be anything from an enamel baking pan to a piece of glass or a standard artist's palette. Use the palette as a surface to flow color on and use the brush to mix colors and to get the paints to the proper consistency. Many paints need no mixing and can be used as they come from the jar or tube. (See Chapter 4 for a discussion of paints.)

8. Equipment for painting glass includes tubes of oil paint, brush, masking tape, turpentine, and spar varnish.

There are some incidental items that go a long way toward making glass painting easy. A wire rack for holding brushes (setting them down on surfaces can cause stains) is helpful. You can make the rack from a coat hanger. Another useful gadget is a hand rest, which is nothing more than a board that elevates your hand and wrist above the glass surface so that it is easy for you to apply paint. A medicine dropper is worth its weight in gold, because you can add turpentine and spar varnish to oil paints with it. (Spar varnish makes oil paints water-resistant; turpentine thins and dries them.)

For making patterns (sometimes called cartoons) you will need white cardboard to draw on. Place the cartoon on the table or desk and anchor it in place at each edge with tape. Place the glass to be painted over the cartoon. The weight of the glass will hold the pane in place. You can also use standard white paper to make patterns. I find cardboard easier to use than paper because it holds up better and is easier to handle.

Any kind of tape can be used to anchor patterns to surfaces, but for pattern making with masking tape (see Chapter 5) you will need several thicknesses from ¼″ to 1″. It is easier to have several thicknesses than to cut and patch pieces together when using masking-tape patterns.

Buy a package of single-edged razor blades for scraping dried paint off glass once the glass is painted. The blade comes in handy if you have made errors or simply want to change something in the painted picture. In fact, the razor blade is indispensible. If you want to be very sophisticated, you can also use an X-acto knife for scraping and correcting errors.

Felt-tip marking pencils and pens are excellent for drawing the working design or cartoon; at least use a #2 standard pencil. The idea is to draw heavy lines that are easily seen through the glass.

Background boards are important for glass painting because they are part of many glass pictures. The color and type of board that you select influences the appearance of the complete piece. Dark boards darken colors while white boards lighten them, and there are a variety of boards and colors that you can use.

Chipboard is a brown board made of compressed wood chips. Millboard is very tough and rigid but is usually available only in gray. Bristol board is rigid and durable and comes in a handsome white. Poster board is also rigid and comes in many colors.

You can have a board cut to your specifications or cut it yourself with a mat knife. Bristol and poster board are sold at art shops; other boards can be salvaged from packing material or boxes.

Whether you paint on the surface of the glass or use the reverse method, the board will become a part of the picture, so choose wisely and make some experiments. Paint colors change as you use different-colored boards.

It is generally unnecessary to glue boards in place: simply put them behind the glass and frame. The frame will hold the board in place. If you do frameless paintings that are bonded together with foil at the edges or if you use frame devices such as clip-ons and so forth, it is necessary to put a dab of glue in each corner of the board to hold it in place.

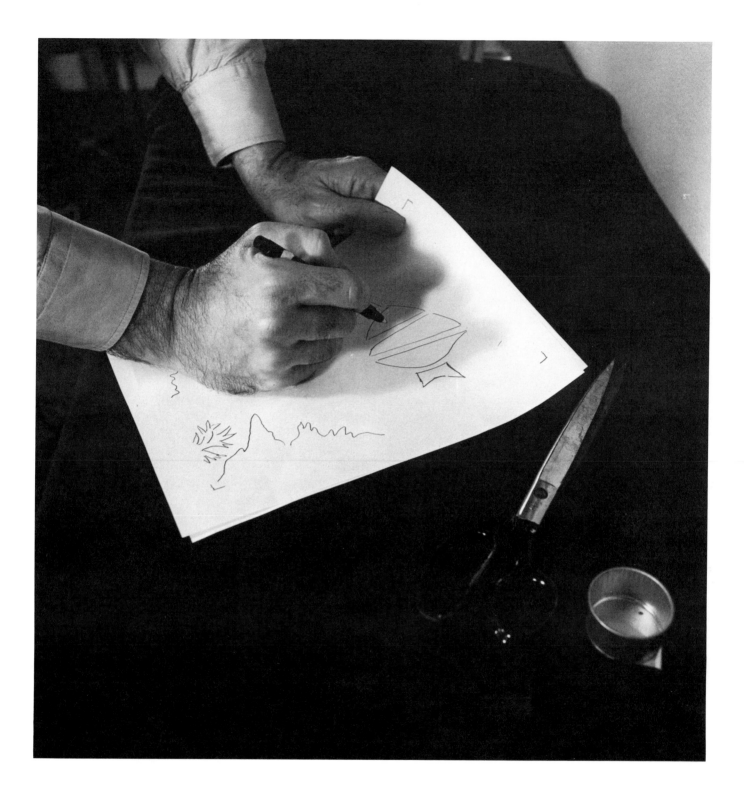

9. The original pattern is outlined with a felt-tip pen.

10. The glass is laid over a cartoon or pattern on a flat surface, and
a fine brush is used to outline the pattern.

PREPARING THE GLASS

Glass must be scrupulously clean before you start painting on it because paint will not hold on soiled or dusty surfaces. Wipe the glass with turpentine; rub it off with a cloth or paper and then wash it in warm water and soap. Rinse and completely dry the glass. To keep the glass clean, hold it by the edges. Whether you cut your own glass or have it done for you, be sure that the edges are smooth. You can remove any sharp edges at home by sanding them under running water with a piece of fine-grained, wettable Carborundum paper.

HANGING DEVICES

In addition to the standard ways to frame paintings there are other hanging devices. The tiny suction-cup hanger is used frequently. It is a plastic cup that, when moistened, can be pressed against a wall or a window; wire is used over the cup and attached to another suction cup on the picture. This is an inexpensive and easy way to put pictures on display.

3. Glass Decoration Unlimited

Glass paintings can be hung on the walls and used in the same ways as paintings on canvas or board. But there are many other uses for glass paintings. Just how you use your finished product depends on your personal tastes; study this chapter for an array of ideas that are sure to please you.

A Gallery of Glass Paintings

Wall-hung Pictures

It is wise to do small sizes of glass pictures because anything over 16" × 20" looks incongruous and heavy. Use a simple painting on glass with a background board or a recessed dimensional picture. Appropriate scenes can include anything from floral designs to landscapes and still lifes.

Easel-back Pictures

For table or desk decoration there is nothing as distinctive as a small, easel-backed glass painting; appropriate frames are sold at frame shops, or you can make your own as detailed in Chapter 7. You can even try your hand at portraits in miniature for charming easel-backed accents.

Windows

You can make handsome stained-glass windows by painting on glass. The size should be small because anything too large is garish and out of scale, but you can use sidelights to frame a door.

Glass Boxes

Clear glass boxes, sold at boutique and department stores, are ideal for painting: a small scene on the inside of the glass makes a handsome addition to a table or desk. The method for box painting is essentially the same as for painting a flat surface of glass.

Plaques

A picture is framed, but a plaque is not. An oval or circular glass painting is very effective as a plaque and can be hung on the wall with various hardware devices or old-fashioned plate hangers.

Silhouette Paintings

Cutting profiles and pictures from paper was popular in England in the 1850s. For glasswork paint in black on the back of a piece of glass. Glass-painted silhouettes look especially effective and nostalgic if done in a circular or oval design and hung on the wall. Silhouettes can also be used as easel-backed pictures.

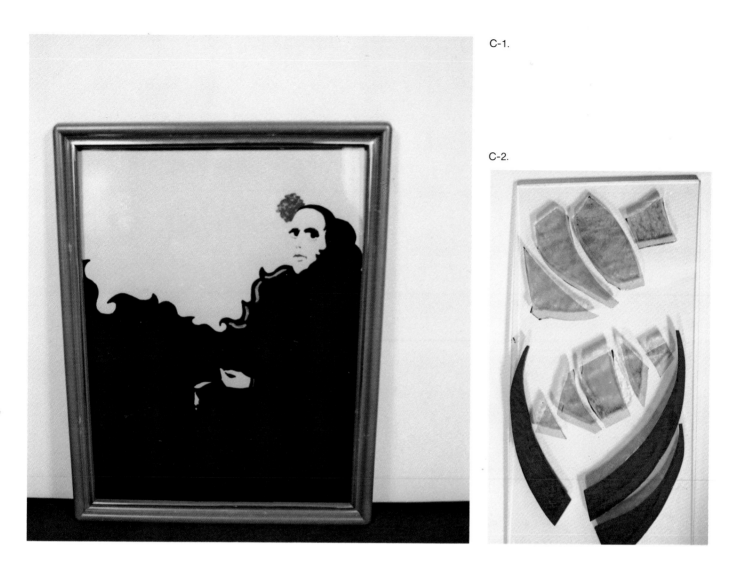

C-1.

C-2.

C-1. Silhouette paintings are highly effective: this one was done with enamels on the reverse side of the glass.

C-2. Glass bonded to glass (in this case stained glass) creates a fanciful fish painting.

C-3. Transparent paint and clear-glass areas are used to create a handsome scene.

C-4. A commercial glass-painted plaque.

C-5. Made with liquid lead and transparent paint, this floral pattern is easy to do and takes only minutes.

C-6. This is not a true stained-glass window but rather consists of liquid lead and transparent paints.

C-7. Oils were used for this daisy picture; with the recessed photograph behind it ready for framing.

C-8. A colorful rainbow for indoor decoration, made with transparent paints and liquid lead.

C-9. A commercial desk-partition-type glass picture is used as a decorative accent.

C-10. A combination of acrylic and transparent paints was used for this bird.

C-11. Inexpensive glass markers created this distinctive flower painting.

C-12. Using a glass jar, the craftsman can decorate to his desire; here transparent paints were used.

C-13. A window pattern painted in acrylics.

C-14. The simple black pattern done in oil is shown against an acrylic painting, ready for framing.

C-15. A handsome simulated-lead glass window done with transparent paint and liquid lead.

C-16. A commercial glass painting with a watercolor background.

C-17. Circles of glass colored with transparent paint and lined with simulated foil make a hanging decoration for a window.

C-3.

C-4.

C-5.

C-6.

C-7.

C-8.

C-9.

C-10.

C-11.

C-12.

C-13.

C-14.

C-15.

C-16.

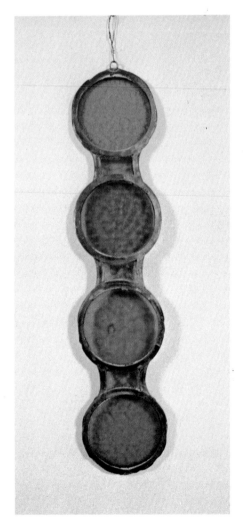

C-17.

Game Boards

Game boards such as checkerboards are easy to paint on glass. You might also want to try other game patterns such as Chinese checkers. Besides being useful painted, game boards make delightful conversation pieces.

Partitions

A full-size glass-painting partition is beyond the scope of this book, but small-scale partitions—say, 16" high—in an accordion-type pattern can be used as dividers or decorative accents on tables or desks. The glass painting becomes a total entity when drawn with appropriate landscapes, seascapes, and so on.

Mirrored Pictures

The combination of mirror and paint makes an effective wall hanging, and you can do this type of picture by following the guidelines in Chapter 8.

Desk Cards and Number Posts

There is no reason why you cannot make a desk plaque of your name by painting on glass. You can also paint your house number on glass.

Stained Glass

The leaded stained-glass windows of yesteryear are very popular today. The authentic leaded-glass window is difficult to make and usually requires a professional, but you can make many types of simulated stained-glass windows using either a lead substitute or the foil method. (These methods are discussed in Chapter 6.)

Dinnerware

Painting clear-glass plates and other kitchen items such as jars is a distinctive way to create something of your own. You can hand-paint motifs or apply spray paint using masking tape to make patterns (see Chapter 5).

Glass Assemblage

Assemblage is not really painting but more like collage. Small pieces of glass are bonded to a clear sheet to create a picture. There is great dimension in glass assemblage, and many distinctive pictures can be made. The craft itself is unique and fun to do.

COMMERCIAL GLASS PAINTINGS

The popularity of painting on glass has resulted in many commercially manufactured decorative-glass products. Unlike the handwork discussed in this book, most of the commercial products are made by the silk-screen method, which results in uniformity and a certain precision. Silk-screen techniques require equipment and special skills for cutting screens; there are several books available on silk screen if you want to pursue this craft.

Some of the commercial products that I have seen recently include various window-hung plaques—the astrological round disk is quite popular. These plaques are attached to window frames; light reflecting through them produces handsome effects. Other items are small stained-glass panes and handsome painted-glass panels for table and desk. The glass panels are either landscape scenes or pictures of animals or flowers. The panels are either single or double and are hinged with adhesive. But to my mind handmade glass paintings are always more handsome and distinctive; they are one-of-a-kind efforts, and they cost much less than commercial panels. Most important, the satisfaction of doing it yourself makes glass painting a totally fascinating and effective way of using your talents.

4. Paints

The equipment for glass painting is not extensive: all you really need is a piece of glass, some paints, and your imagination. As an art or hobby painting on glass can be done by young or old with good results. This book deals with several kinds of painting on flat glass; some of them can also be used for goblets and other round vessels.

THE BASICS

Most of the color designs seen on glass bowls, cups, or functional items are applied by firing at specific temperatures. Fired-glass paints are permanent, but the process requires an expensive kiln, space, and extensive knowledge of temperatures and chemicals.

The unfired process—that is, painting designs on glass—is more suitable for the average person. Although the paint is not as permanent as fired paint, it is an excellent, inexpensive way of decorating glass. Since most decorative pictures, panels, boxes, and so on need little washing, the unfired process is fine.

Painting on glass differs from painting on canvas or paper in that glass is a nonabsorbent material. The paint is pushed into place or flowed on rather than applied with brushstrokes. The strokes must be delicate but defined, and clear spaces are frequently used as part of the total picture.

Before you select a pattern or start a painting, practice on some scrap glass. You will immediately see that it is easy to draw a straight line; it is the curved lines that require experience. Get the feeling of the hard, glossy surface under the paintbrush: it is slick and slippery, more like skating on ice than walking on a pavement. But, in spite of all the differences between glass painting and painting on porous surfaces, glass painting is easy because, once the paint dries, you can scrape away any errors with a razor blade or X-acto knife.

HOW TO DO IT

Once you have decided on a pattern—whether from this book (see Chapter 9), a magazine picture, or whatever—for a painting on glass, trace the picture or pattern onto cardboard or paper. Anchor the pattern to a flat, level surface and place a piece of glass over it. Lightly paint the pattern on the glass or make a light tracing with a grease pencil. Small paintings on glass are generally better than large paintings, because the small size is more intimate and charming and more readily lends itself to glass.

Depending upon the type of paint that you select, prepare it to the proper consistency. If one color is to shade into another, apply the second color while the first is still wet. If one color is to be applied over another *without* shading or is to be next to another color, wait until the first is dry.

Apply paint as thinly as possible and take your time. Guard against smudging and overlap. Be patient. If you make a mistake, carefully wipe away the paint with a rag or cloth.

TYPES OF PAINT

There are several types of paint that can be used for glasswork. Oil paint is the most difficult to use on flat glass because of its consistency. It can be neither too thick nor too thin and requires some practice sessions. Several enamels are now available in many colors and can readily be applied to glass. Acrylics are rubber-based paints that come in many opaque colors. Translucent paints or stains are available in only a limited amount of colors but are unexcelled for glass painting. Glass markers and metallic paints are other media that you can use. Spray paint is also available and has its uses.

Acrylics

Acrylics are opaque paints that can be used dramatically in glass painting. They are water-based, unlike oils, which is an advantage in cleaning up. They are less smelly than oils, but their major advantage for glass painting is perhaps that they dry quickly. Acrylics are easier to apply to glass than oils or enamels and create a flat, opaque finish.

To work with acrylics, draw the design with grease pencil on the surface of the glass, turn the glass over on white paper or board, and fill in the pattern areas with paint—in other words, apply acrylics in reverse on the glass. Apply the paint in single strokes so that the strokes will not show. Even with the most perfect application, however, some brushstrokes may show, but, once the backing is put in place, they are minimized.

Try several different types of backing; each will give a somewhat different effect. Start with a white background board, then try a blue or orange board: results vary. Experiment until you find the most appropriate background.

You can also use acrylics for surface painting by placing the glass over a pattern and painting the outline forms without tracing a grease-pencil line.

Oils

Oils are the paints that are used for painting on canvas and, if you are already proficient in oil painting, you will find a new dimension when you try them on glass. Oils are available in tubes in a multitude of colors at art stores, and, unlike acrylic and enamel, which are generally used as they come from the tube or bottle, they are usually mixed to create the desired color.

Oils are more difficult to apply to glass than acrylic or stains, because they have to have an almost perfect consistency: the brush must retain paint to complete a stroke without going dry. If oils are too runny or too thick, they just will not work well. As advised earlier, mix oils with spar varnish to hasten drying and with turpentine if they require thinning.

You can apply oil on the surface of the glass or turn the glass over for a reverse painting to achieve more dimension and lucidity.

11. Acrylics were used for this layered painting; they are opaque
and easy to apply.

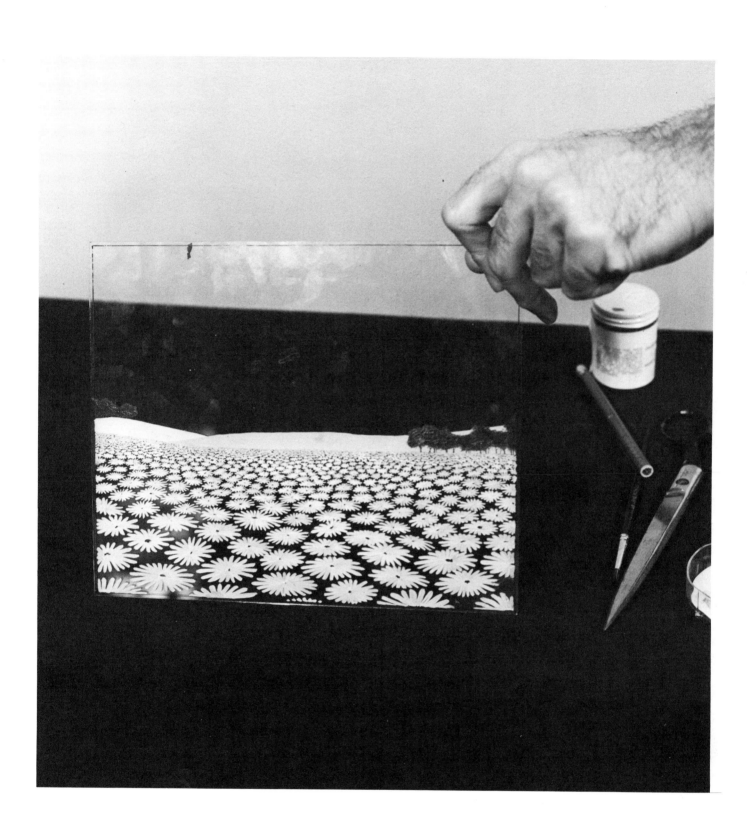

12. Oils were used to paint on the reverse side of this glass.

For your first project use a somewhat large piece of glass—say, 9″ × 12″—that is fairly thick (³⁄₁₆″) for greater dimension. Select a picture and trace it on white paper (or make your own sketch); outline the areas to get your pattern. When the sketch is completed, run over it once again with a black felt-tip pen so that it is clearly visible. Lay a sheet of glass over the traced pattern or original sketch. Decide on an outline color: for example, a dark green works well in a nature scene. Mix the oil paint on the palette with spar varnish and a few drops of turpentine and draw the outline with a #0 brush. When the paint has set, apply fill-in colors with #1 and #2 brushes. Let each color set before applying the next. When the complete picture is finished, tape the edges of the glass with a thin border of narrow adhesive-backed copper, gold, bronze, or silver tape.

The picture is now ready for framing or mounting; you can install it in a regular picture frame with a suitably colored background board and frame it as you would an ordinary painting, or you can use an easel frame or make your own, as described in Chapter 7. If the background color of the easel is not gray or white, drape the easel with another color of fabric.

Enamels

Sometimes called poster or bulletin paints, enamels work well on glass; they come in bright colors and have a shiny brilliance that makes them suitable for floral designs. Enamels can be used as they come from the bottle, so no mixing is necessary. If a large area of paint is required on a glass painting, enamels are the best choice. These paints are opaque and can be used on the surface of the glass (after making a pattern with a grease pencil) or on the reverse side. A front-surface painting can merely be turned over to get the reverse quality, but, of course, the design will be reversed as well.

Enamels take longer to dry than acrylics but in general are fine for glass painting.

Transparent Paints

Transparent paints come in jars and in several colors; they are specifically designed for glass painting and offer many avenues of expression. Because they are transparent, paintings are best used against windows where natural light enters to create a striking effect. Transparent paints, sometimes called stains, are so easy to use that even a beginner can get good results, and they are especially appropriate for landscape and flower pictures. With transparent paints there is little difference between painting on the surface of the glass or using the paint on the reverse side. The overall product looks the same.

I use Politec transparent paints. Your area may carry different brands—just ask for transparent paints for glass.

To use transparent paints, make your line design of the scene you want on paper with a black felt-tip marker. Draw the design to exact size and scale. Anchor the pattern to a flat table with tape and place the glass over it. For this type of painting use glass such as ⅛″ or ³⁄₁₆″ crystal. Outline the pattern on glass with a suitable color—blue or black.

Use a painting rack for the glass jars of transparent paint, because they tend to tip over if you are not as agile as a deer. A board with suitable holes can be made easily and really comes in handy. You will also want some flat and some fine pointed sable brushes, such as a #00 for the fine outline work and touches and a #1 for filling in areas. Apply each color separately and let each color dry before applying the next.

When the painting is finished and thoroughly dry, it can be framed in various ways. The backing can be a pastel or flat-white board. Or use the transparent painting against a window to get great color as light passes through it. Against solid colors such as boards the colors of transparent paints are not as vivid.

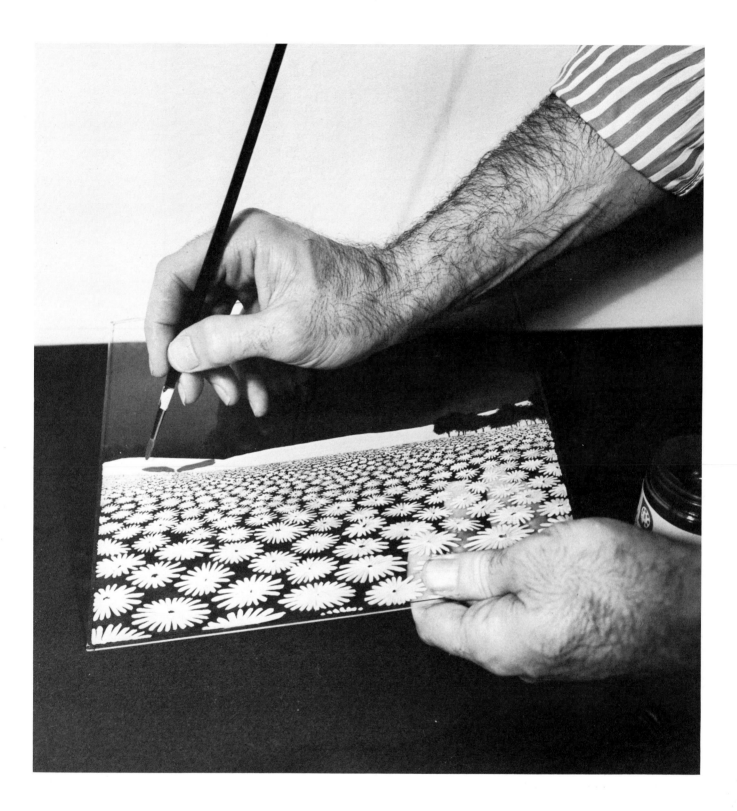

13. Enamel is used for highlights on the surface of a reverse painting.

14. This free-form flower was done with transparent paints and
liquid lead.

Glass Markers

Inexpensive and available in many colors, glass markers are extremely easy to use. These felt-tip pens are available in several point thicknesses from fine to broad. The ¼" points are fine for most glass paintings. Applying the color is extremely easy—like writing—so this is an excellent medium for beginners. The colors are transparent and slightly lighter in tone than standard glass stains. These markers come in permanent or washable colors; permanent is best because it gives a better tint.

Painting with these felt-tip markers is very much the same as for most glass painting. Outline the pattern or scene and fill in with color. The markers are somewhat touchy to use because you cannot redo a surface of paint, so it will take some expertise before you can reach perfection. Still, this is an inexpensive and quick way to make almost instant pictures and decorations.

Metallic Paints

Metallic (gilt) paints work beautifully on glass because they transmit light: a gold or silver metallic edge will make a line glow on a glass painting. Metallic paints are sold in many hardware and art stores under the trade name Liquid Leaf. This brush-on paint comes in silver, gold, copper, and brass colors and is excellent for finishing touches. Use a separate brush for the metallic paints and clean it with a product called Eylene (at the same stores as the paints).

Apply metallic paint as smoothly and as carefully as you can with a fine-pointed brush. Try not to paint over it, but, after it dries—about 6 hours—you can apply a second coat. Use a #00 or #0 brush for metallic paints.

Spray Paints

The most personal glass paintings are done by hand, using brushes and standard paints, but there are other ways to make patterns, and the most flexible is to use masking tape and spray paints in cans. The method works well for geometrical designs and other straight-line techniques; it is somewhat more difficult for curved patterns.

To make a masking-tape pattern, outline your design with tape on a clear piece of glass and press tightly so that the paint does not seep underneath. Cover the rest of the glass surface with newspaper so that specks of paint will not spatter in unwanted areas. Apply one color at a time; let each color dry before applying others.

The masking-tape technique works beautifully on clear-glass plates, which are sold in most furnishings stores. You can create your own lovely designs that are really distinctive. Apply the paint to the underside of the plates so that it does not get scratched. Remember that hand-painted dinnerware of this type cannot be put in a dishwasher: it must be washed with a light hand, or the paint may come off. With care, however, it is quite acceptable.

If you decide to add color designs to bowls, cups, or glasses, the painted design is applied to the outside of the glass. This is a unique way to put your very own special designs on glassware and have lots of fun at the same time.

15. Glass markers are also easy to paint with: the design can be done
in minutes.

38

16. The completed glass-marker painting.

17. Metallic gold leaf is used to highlight a silhouette painting.

PROTECTIVE FINISHES

Most decorative glass paintings done in unfired colors, especially those painted on the back of the glass and protected by boards, last many years if they are not mishandled or washed with abrasives. Once the paint has dried, paintings can be dusted or lightly washed in warm water to keep them clean.

If your decorative glass paintings are handled frequently or given undue use, you might want to protect them with one of the many clear acrylic finishes. These finishes are sold in aerosol cans and pump jars under various trade names and are called acrylic clear-spray coatings; they are moisture- and smudge-proof. Follow the directions on the can to the letter and always use the spray in a well-ventilated place.

If you are dubious about using a spray coating, protect glass paintings with one of the clear finishes that are sold in cans and applied with a brush like ordinary paint. I use a product called Deft, but there are many others available. Some of these work well but some can ruin oil paints, so read all labels carefully.

A very simple way of protecting pictures is to use a clear acetate sheet (it looks like Saran wrap) over the surface of the glass. It is pressed and wrapped around the glass and usually holds in place without glues—if necessary, a dab of glue can be used.

5. Painting On Glass

There are many techniques for painting on glass. Each method can be used by itself—for example, a simple abstract or geometric silhouette for a small window or partition, an oil painting, a stained glass, or a painting done with transparent paints. This chapter discusses these basic techniques: (1) reverse painting on clear glass, (2) silhouette, (3) layered-glass painting, (4) painting on glassware, (5) recessed paintings, and (6) overlaying paint methods. (Simulated stained-glass paintings are covered in Chapter 6.)

REVERSE PAINTING ON GLASS

Why paint on the back of glass when you can paint on the front? There are several advantages. A reverse painting, once framed, is more permanent than a surface work, as there is little chance of scratching it. Painting the reverse side of glass also creates a dimensional quality that is very handsome. The reverse method achieves a look of brillance: glass is a reflective material, so looking through it creates a unique effect.

Popular in the early 1900s, especially for clocks, a reverse painting is always framed and thus protected from dust, soot, and accidental scrubbing by some household helper. The reverse-painting technique is generally used with opaque paint and also works well with a photograph or graphic-type background placed a few inches from the glass. This provides a still more dimensional quality and creates an almost box-art-type picture that is quite stunning.

For reverse painting use a heavier glass than is normally used for surface painting. A ⅛″ or ³⁄₁₆″ thickness works very well. Remember that, when you turn over the glass, the pattern will be reversed. Paint highlights and shadows on the glass first instead of applying them as finished strokes. After these details dry, do the fill-in painting and the backgrounds.

The reverse method of painting is best for oils, enamels, or acrylics. Once the painting is framed, there is little chance of scratching it off. It is an easy way to achieve striking results, because light passing through the glass painting creates a unique effect. There is little benefit in using the reverse method with transparent paints and glass markers.

SILHOUETTES

Silhouettes generally do not lend themselves to large paintings on clear window glass, but they are decorative and add great charm to small windows or dividers. To make a silhouette painting, draw the pattern on a sheet of white paper with a black felt-tip pen—copy a geometrical or abstract pattern from a magazine or make your own. The pattern should be executed clearly and crisply with no jagged lines. Tape the pattern to a flat board or table and lay the pane of glass over the pattern. The glass size should match the pattern size with a ½" or 1" clear border if desired. The glass can be taped into place over the pattern, but this is not necessary, because the weight of the glass will hold the pattern in place.

Black enamel is used for this project. Use the paint as it comes from the jar. To start the painting, use a 3" board to rest your palm on (you have probably seen painters doing this). Trace the outline with black paint. If the brush accumulates paint, dip it into turpentine from time to time and dry it on paper toweling. When the outline work is finished, let it dry. Apply the fill-in paint with a #3 brush liner. Let this coat dry and repaint to fill in any thin areas. When the second coat is dry, see if there are any jagged lines. If so, gently scrape away any mistakes with a single-edged razor blade. If you want to paint on the back of the glass— this effect is desirable for silhouettes—remember that the pattern will be reversed, so take this into account in making the original pattern.

Instead of black paint any dark-colored opaque paint can be used for the silhouette painting. The pane can be installed against a window glass with thin moldings. If you are making a divider, paint four or five panels with the same design, depending on how large the divider is to be. A typical divider screen has five panels in an accordion-type frame; set the divider on a counter between a kitchen and dining room for an interesting effect.

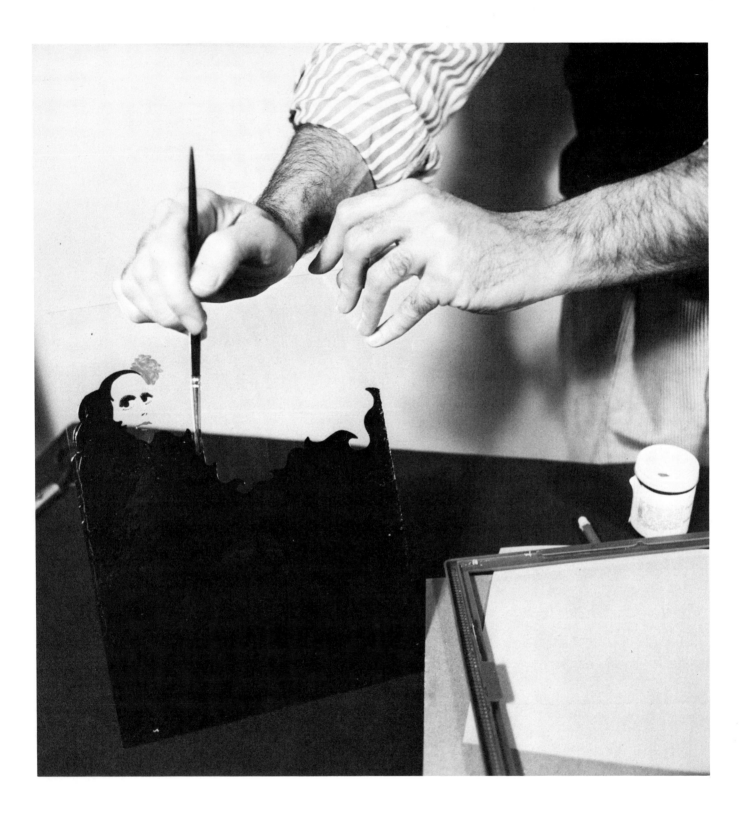

18. A silhouette is painted on the reverse side of the glass.

19. The completed silhouette framed.

LAYERED PICTURES

This section explains how to layer several pieces of glass, each with one part of the pattern, together like a sandwich to create a very unique picture. This is not to be confused with overlaying paint on paint.

For this project you will need three pieces of glass cut to exactly the same size; a good size is 8″ × 10″. Select a suitable pattern, one with at least four colors and that is in sections—for example, flowers, leaves, and buds. One pane of glass will show flowers, the second leaves, and the third buds.

Make three separate patterns of each element in the design; place the first pattern under the glass and apply paint to cover the object. Set aside the glass. Place the second pattern on the table, tape it in place, and put the glass on top. Do the painting and set aside the glass. Place the third pattern on the table and follow the same procedure.

When all the paint on the three pieces of glass has dried, assemble the complete picture. Cut out 12 pieces of acetate ½″ × ½″ square. These are used in each corner of the three pieces of glass to allow air to flow between the panes and to protect the paint from being scraped off by the adjoining piece of glass.

To glue the glass panes together, apply glue to the acetate squares in each corner and carefully lay the second and third panes next to the first. Stack the painting so that the three pieces of glass are properly aligned along the edges and on the pattern. Check the original pattern as you work.

To complete a picture done in the front of the glass, place a piece of acetate (sold at art stores) over the entire surface to protect the top painting; glue it in place at each corner. The painting is now ready for framing, or it can be bonded at the edges with aluminum or brass stripping and wall-hung with suitable hangers (sold at hardware stores).

20. Starting a three-layer painting.

21. When the paint is dry, a ½″ square piece of double-faced tape is
placed in each corner to form a cushion and separate panes.

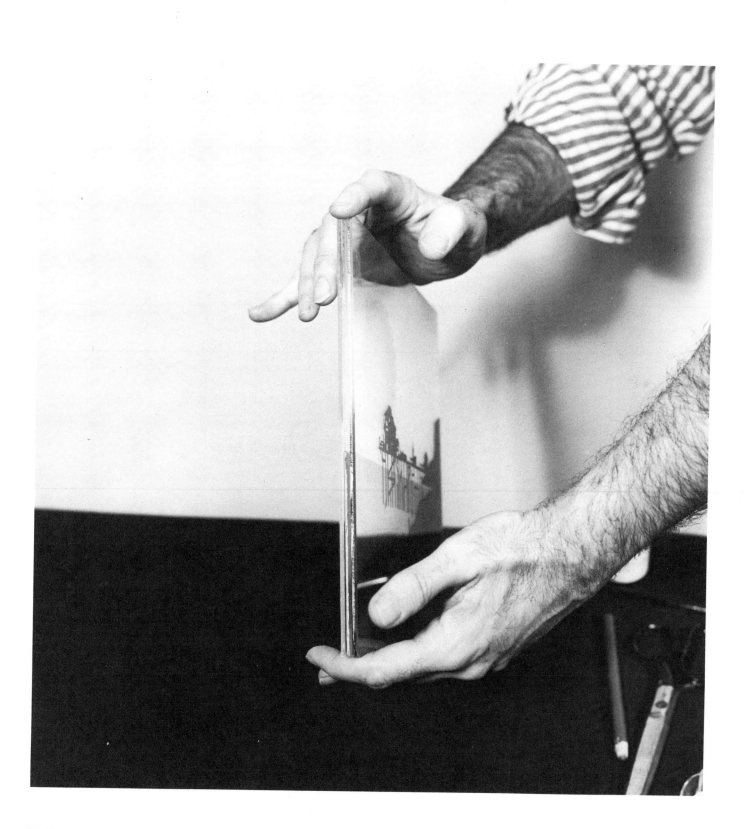

22. Three panes of the painting are layered.

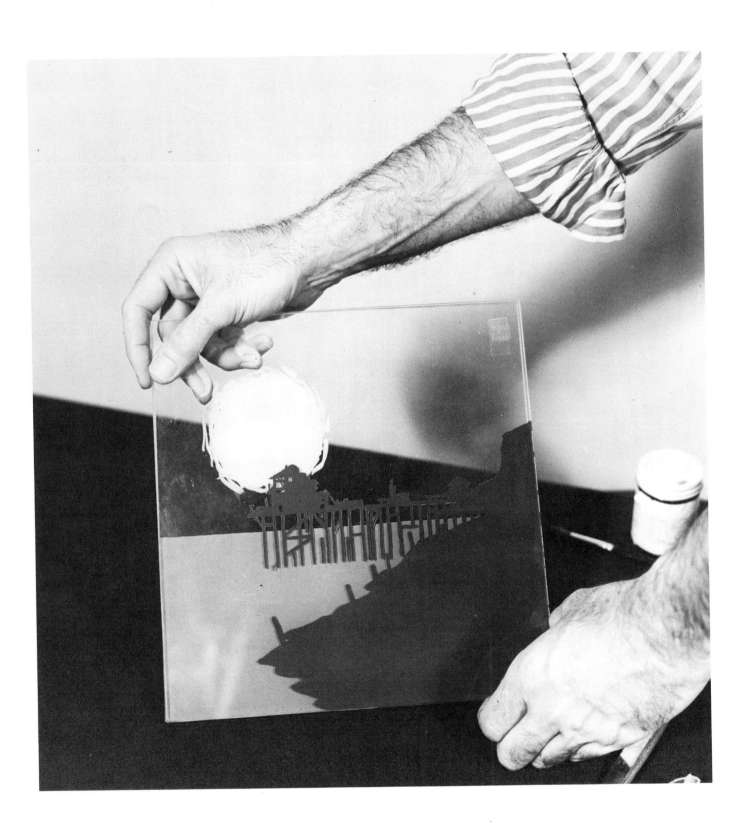

23. The finished three-layer painting.

PAINTING ON GLASSWARE

Colored-glass bottles or clear-glass vases can be made into handsome, distinctive, and unique pieces by painting floral or bird motifs on the outside surface. Floral designs, which are especially effective on glass bottles and vases, can be applied with oils or enamel: the more delicate the tracery, the more handsome the overall effect. To make a pattern on a glass bottle or vase, use a grease pencil for outlining. Sharpen the tip of the pencil to a fine point with a razor blade. Outline the design with a #00 brush and fill in the design with thicker brushes.

Remember that painted bottles and vases are unfired: washing or scrubbing them with abrasives will remove the design, so clean them by dusting with a dry cloth.

24. Starting a free-form geometric pattern for a plateware painting
with masking tape.

25. The masking tape for the triangular pattern is in place, and
newspapers cover the rest of the plate.

26. Allow the spray paint to dry.

27. Remove the tape.

28. The finished pattern; you can add to it to make a complete pattern.

RECESSED PICTURES

By its very nature glass has a dimensional quality that other painting surfaces do not have, giving the hobbyist an opportunity to create almost luminescent pictures. And there are many different ways to achieve further dimensional effects.

Use background photographs, colored boards, or two painted surfaces, spacing the surfaces 1" apart. There is fantastic adventure in painting on glass, and how you put it all together is half the fun. Some of the examples in this book will get your imagination going.

Say that you have painted a scene on glass, that it is dry, and that you want to mount it for framing. You can apply a board directly to the back of the glass, which is especially effective with acrylics because the board produces a darker color by shutting out the light. To achieve a different effect, leave an air space of 1" between the painting and the background board. On the background board paint a picture that complements the glass painting. For example, paint a tree landscape across the length of the glass and on the board paint hills, sky, and grass in another color and medium. When you put the board behind the glass, you achieve a very pleasing dimensional picture. And if you become very proficient at glass painting, you can superimpose two separate images: one on the glass, backed up by another one on the board.

The recessed method can also be used with transparent paints to produce a startling effect. The paints should be highlighted with either white or very dark, almost black, boards as a background. A colored board will give your picture a totally different effect. For example, paint a flower with transparent paint on the glass and place a white board 1" behind it. Or try a black board: the character of the pastel flower will be completely changed.

PHOTOGRAPH BACKGROUNDS

Another way of dramatizing your glass painting is to back it up with a photograph. The photograph can be applied to the back of the glass, but it will be more impressive if you recess the photograph 1" or so directly behind the glass.

The photograph may be of any subject, but it must be appropriate to the painting. Or approach it the other way: do the painting first and then look for the right photograph. A black-and-white photograph works better than a colored one. Make sure that your glass painting complements the photograph by painting delicate traceries: broad areas of paint do not work well against a photograph. For example, use a black-and-white photograph of a nude and paint delicate foliage or flowers on the glass. Place the photograph and the glass 1" apart for a dazzling effect, a dimensional quality that ordinary canvas paintings lack.

OVERLAYERING

Still another way to achieve a dimensional quality in a glass painting is to use the surface method of overlaying paints—that is, paint a flower, for example, and, when it is dry, paint another flower half way over the original one. This subject can then be backed up by painting foliage through or over both paintings. The effect is highly dramatic and dimensional, but you should first become proficient at simple painting on glass before attempting the layering method.

You can use many combinations of paint for layering. For example, you can use transparent and acrylic paints, oils backed with transparent stains, and so forth. Experiment until you find the combination you like best.

There are four ways to achieve dimension in glass painting: (1) to paint each of several pieces of glass, (2) to place a recessed painting behind the glass, (3) to use a photograph behind the glass, and (4) to apply paint over paint (each color must be dry before overlaying). You will find that each type of dimensional painting creates a different effect, and it is exciting to experiment and see the final results.

29. A watercolor background board is used with glass painting in the recessed method.

30. The background board is in place behind the painting, ready for framing.

31. A transparent-paint flower is used against a watercolor.

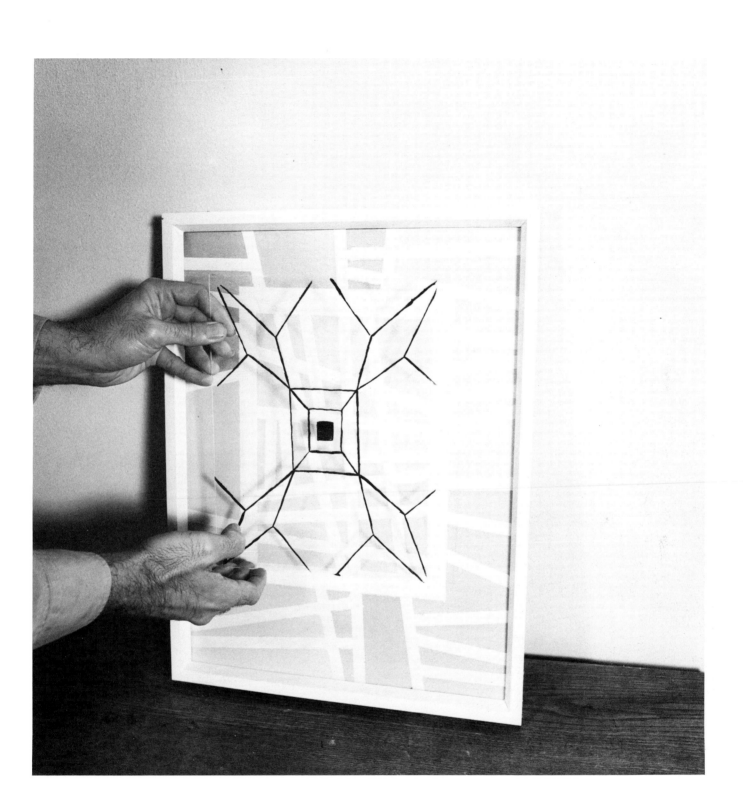

32. A geometric design is used to enhance a painting.

6. Stained-glass Effects

Stained-glass windows, window ornaments, and lamps have become increasingly popular in the last few years because stained glass adds elegance and color and offers the hand-hewn look missing in today's houses. There are several methods of making stained-glass objects, ranging from authentic leaded-glass processes to glass bonded with epoxy resins and to flux and soldering techniques. These methods are covered fully in many books, so they are not discussed here.

The stained-glass effects described in this chapter are done with inexpensive simulated techniques that you can learn at home. One method is to apply imitation or liquid lead to the glass and to paint the glass with transparent colors; another method is to cut out pieces of stained glass, to bond them to a clear sheet of glass, and to use grout to simulate lead.

TRANSPARENT-PAINT STAINED GLASS

This method is the simplest way to make stained glass. Simulated lead (black in color) comes in a tube (ask your dealer for liquid lead); one brand is called Dam-It. Use the lead to define the colored areas. Do shake the tube thoroughly, even though the instructions do not instruct you to. If you do not shake the tube, the liquid escapes as you apply it.

Use clear glass for stained-glass work. Make a pattern—floral, abstract, or whatever. Because you are not making a commercial unit, it is not necessary to be exact in your design. You can also just draw the pattern on a piece of paper, since no glass cutting is involved in this process. Make the pattern full-scale on paper. Use a black marking pencil; once the sectioning is done, write the names of the colors that you want to use. Study old stained-glass windows to see how colors can be arranged for a handsome effect. For example, beautiful clarets, reds, and pinks would make a stunning window, but placing reds next to yellows would most likely be garish. But this is a matter of personal taste, so no rigid color combinations are specified here.

33. Pieces of stained glass with grout in between them simulate
a leaded window.

After the pattern is made, pin or tape it to a level board or any white-surfaced background. Set a piece of glass, the same size as the pattern, over it. Apply the simulated lead in ribbon fashion to the dark-sectioned lines. Apply it slowly but evenly: your goal is to create straight or curved lines without kinks or bends. Some practice might be necessary.

When the simulated-lead lines are done, let them dry. After they are dry, start applying the paints to the clear sections. Work slowly and carefully. The leaded lines are somewhat raised, so you do not want the lead and the paints to overlap. Paint the transparent paint evenly and in broad strokes to avoid streaking. Use red-sable brushes. A broad brush is fine for large areas, but for filling in against the lead use a #000 brush.

Do not try to mix paints on the glass—in fact, any mixing should be avoided. Use the paint as it comes from the jar, although you can thin it with paint thinner if it is too thick. Your paint should have a medium consistency and should never be runny.

COLORED-GLASS STAINED GLASS

This method of making stained glass is somewhat more difficult than the first, but it is certainly not beyond the capabilities of the average person. Several small pieces of stained glass are bonded with epoxy to one clear-glass pane. The pieces are filled in with grout to simulate leaded-glass skeletons.

Make three patterns of your design. Put a sheet of paper over a sheet of carbon paper over another sheet of paper over another piece of carbon paper, all on top of a piece of slick cardboard. You should have two sheets of paper, two pieces of carbon paper, and the cardboard, which will give you three patterns. Draw your pattern carefully. Tack down the paper, carbon paper, and cardboard at each corner on a flat surface. Now draw the pattern with a lead pencil. Use a level surface for working, make sure that there is no slippage, and number each space that represents a piece of glass.

Separate the papers and cardboard after tracing. The cardboard pattern is the cutting pattern, so place it on the table. Put a piece of stained glass over the cardboard pattern and attach the corners with masking tape. With a grease pencil carefully mark the pattern on the glass. Remove the cardboard pattern and care-

fully cut out the stained-glass pieces. Cut out the cardboard pieces with an X-acto knife. Tape the cardboard pieces to the back of a pane of clear glass.

Position each piece of stained glass over the clear glass to ensure that all shapes and colors match correctly. Remove each piece of glass and sand the edges to remove sharp slivers and to take off some glass edges.

Remove the cardboard pieces from the second pane of glass and clean and dry the glass. Tape the paper pattern to the board and tape the glass sheet securely to the drawing with masking tape; extend it ¼" around all edges of the perimeter. Spread epoxy thinly and evenly over the back of each piece of stained glass and place a spot of epoxy on the clear glass where each stained-glass piece is to be set. Press each piece firmly into place on the clear glass; the paper pattern underneath is your guide. This bonding process must be done with precision. Wear gloves and get ready to mix the epoxy. Buy the epoxy and hardener at an arts-and-crafts-store; use products such as Elmer's epoxy cement or Thermoset resin-and-hardener kit. Follow the directions carefully because they vary somewhat from manufacturer to manufacturer. Mix the resin and hardener until they are absolutely smooth.

If epoxy oozes from under the glass pieces into the crevices, try to scrape it away with a toothpick or razor blade; use an epoxy solvent if necessary. The areas between the pieces of glass should be clean so that grout can be applied later. Always wear rubber gloves to protect your hands and try to work in a well-ventilated place. Do not be alarmed if you get epoxy on the glass, because it can be removed with solvent when it is rubbery. Once the epoxy hardens, however, it cannot be removed, so do your cleaning right away. When all the glass pieces are bonded, let the panels dry for at least two days.

Mix black or white grout and add water to make a sticky paste. With a spatula knife work the grout into all crevices until it is even with the surface of the glass. Clean off the surface grout right away before it hardens.

Once the pane of glass is completed, it can replace an existing windowpane. Or just hang it in front of a window as a unique decoration—use one of the attaching devices sold at hardware stores.

GLASS ASSEMBLAGE

An assemblage (the term for glass-on-glass pictures), which is similar to but different from stained-glass work, is a unique and challenging way of using glass. Instead of using abstract designs, as in stained glass, natural scenes are generally used. The motif, whether flower or bird, is sectioned in glass pieces and assembled on glass. There is infinitely more cutting involved with this method of gluing small pieces of glass to a sheet of glass, but the results are more dramatic.

For bonded glass-on-glass pictures use simple patterns and few colors. Three colors for a complete picture work well. As you become more experienced, you can try more colors and more challenging patterns. To create a fragment pattern, outline the pattern in the standard way. If you want a bird or flower, for example, make a solid pattern and section it into three or four pieces, keeping the basic image in context. The space between the glass pieces helps to create the dimensional effect: one solid piece of glass—say, a flower bonded to a glass surface—would not have the impact of several fragmented pieces that compose an entire flower.

For glass-on-glass assemblage you will need stained glass, one piece of sheet glass, and a bonding material such as epoxy.

Cutting the Pattern

Draw two patterns of what you want—a bird, an insect, a landscape, and so on. Trace the original pattern on white paper. Put carbon paper under the white paper and retrace the same pattern on white cardboard. Be sure to tape the corners of the paper pattern to ensure an exact match. From the cardboard pattern cut out pieces of stained glass. Follow the cutting rules outlined in Chapter 1. When all the pieces are cut, lay the clear pane of glass over the paper pattern and tape it in place.

Blend the epoxy on a scrap piece of glass; mix only a small amount at one time. Spread the epoxy thinly with a paste brush on the underside of each stained-glass fragment. Press the stained-glass pieces firmly into place over the outline beneath the glass base. Pick up very small pieces of stained glass with tweezers to avoid getting epoxy on your hands. When all the pieces are in place, let the epoxy dry overnight. Unlike the methods described at the beginning of this chapter, which involve grout or simulated lead, in assemblage the glass pieces are placed closely together, only ⅛" apart, and lead or grout is not used.

Bond hangers to the top of each corner of the clear glass or put the picture on a white easel back for desk or table use. You can also add a fine line of metallic foil around all the edges to act as a frame.

Pattern Making

The secret of the glass-on-glass method is to make the pattern properly: there should be enough fragments so that, when they are put together, they look like a whole picture. Do not cut too many pieces, however, or the picture might resemble a jigsaw puzzle. Either leave space between the fragments, as in the example, or place them together. As you go along, you will become more proficient. A very interesting variation results from adding small ¼" glass mosaic tiles (sold at craft shops) as a foreground or background. Just place the tiles randomly.

34. Two patterns are made (using carbon paper) for the glass-on-glass bonded picture, one for the pattern, as shown, and one as a template for cutting the pieces.

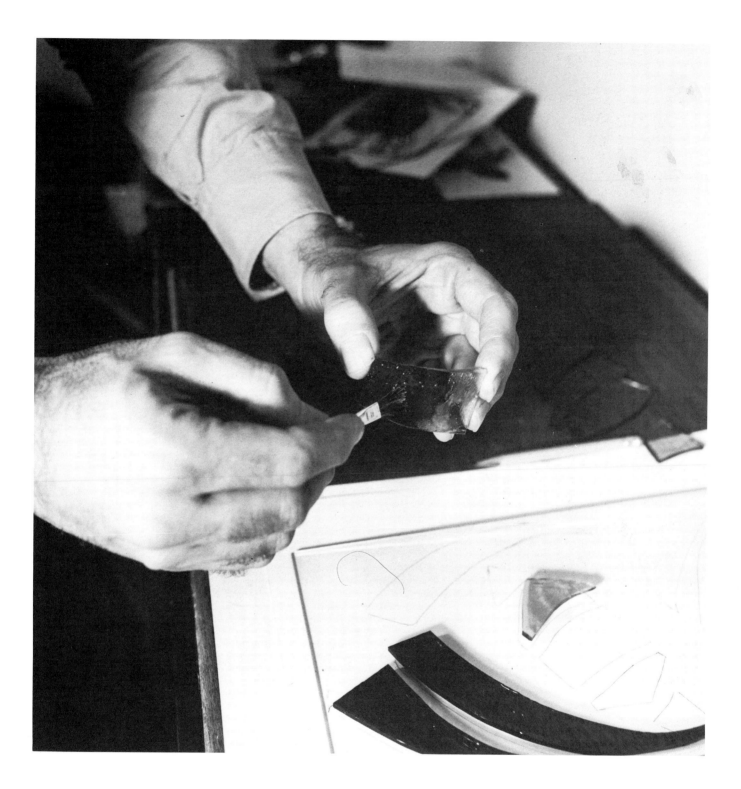

35. Epoxy is applied to the glass pieces to adhere them to the clear
pane.

36. Setting the glass pieces in place to make the painting.

37. The glass-on-glass painting is almost complete.

38. Be sure to brush both the back of the fragmented pieces of glass
and the clear glass with epoxy.

39. The completed glass-on-glass picture.

7. Finishing Touches

Many glass pictures can be left unframed by using the frame hangers sold at art-supply stores and frame shops. A frame hanger is a device that supports the top and bottom of the glass and can be hooked into a wall. Glass pictures can also be set on easels or used in a fold—that is, separated but still adhered with epoxy and opened to stand by themselves.

Dimensional glass pictures, in which a background board is either fixed to the glass or a short distance away from it, need special framing. You can have this done at frame shops, but it is much less expensive to do it yourself, and you can control the effect you want. Framing paintings on glass is very important; this chapter explores various ways to put your work on display.

MOUNTING

The simple wire top-and-bottom-rod picture frame puts a picture on display but without a frame. It is an effective but not very glamorous way of hanging a painting. For small glass pictures where simplicity is wanted, however, it is a very satisfactory way of putting your work on show.

If you have a single pane of painted glass, you can merely attach an easel-type backing to it, which makes the painting suitable for table or desk display. You can also make the back yourself. Transfer an outline of the pane size to a piece of composition, Masonite, or poster board. Cut out the outline with a mat knife. With the mat knife cut a portion of the back of the board at the center to serve as the easel.

The board backing is now ready to be applied to the glass. Dab clear epoxy around the edges of the glass and press the board onto the glass. To finish off the easel "frame," wrap the edges securely with a thin piece of gold or silver foil. Use a ¼" ribbon of self-adhesive mastic tape to secure the foil.

If you have two glass panels and want to join them, use clear-colored double-backed masking tape along the inside edges of each piece of glass. Press the two panes together and open them up. The glass panels will stand by themselves for table or desk decoration.

HANGING DEVICES

In addition to the standard ways to frame paintings there are other hanging devices. The tiny suction-cup hanger is used frequently. It is a plastic cup that, when moistened, can be pressed against a wall or a window; wire is used over the cup and attached to another suction cup on the picture. This is an inexpensive and easy way to put pictures on display.

FRAMES

Most glass paintings are unframed, either used as table and desk ornaments or hung on the wall or window. But, some glass paintings—those rendered in the dimensional process against a photographed or painted background—should be framed.

You can buy frames; there are many different types available at stores. Some frames come in kits with four pieces of molding that you assemble yourself, and others are standard picture frames with glass. But it is less expensive to make your own frames from picture moldings (sold at frame shops) or builder's molding (sold at lumberyards).

Because there are so many possible ways of framing a glass painting, the following method is only one basic technique. You can devise your own variations once you know the general method. To make a frame, you need a miter box, which will give you an accurate 45° angle at each end of the moldings. Measure the four molding strips and add on twice the width of the molding strip plus 1″ to each piece as a margin for error in sawing.

Cut the molding at a 90° angle, set the miter box and saw for a right-hand 45° angle cut, and make the cuts. When you have cut one end of each of the four moldings with a right-hand 45° angle cut, make all the left-hand 45°-angle cuts.

Secure the ends of the moldings with epoxy, nails, or a combination of both. Drill holes in the back of the frame for eyelets to hold the picture wire so that you can hang the painting.

40. You can buy ready-made frames such as this one.

41. A miter box is used to make angle cuts on frames.

42. The frames are glued and nailed at the corners.

43. Finished joint of the frame.

8. Painting On Mirrors

Once you have mastered some of the techniques for painting on clear glass, you might want to try your hand at the fascinating craft of painting on mirrors. Mirrors painted with contemporary designs are available commercially and are indeed handsome, but they are expensive. You can do your own and choose from an infinite variety of patterns rather than only what is available.

For mirror painting the best pattern is a silhouette-type contemporary design: it creates a dimensional and handsome picture. Consider simple motifs, such as a border line and a single bird or a handsome flower in one corner, so that most of the mirror is visible for viewing. The border acts as a frame to add decorative flair to the piece. There are infinite patterns, but the simple ones look best and are the easiest for the beginner to tackle.

BASIC METHOD

There are actually several ways to paint on glass: commercial products utilize a silk-screen process whereby the color pattern is screened before the glass is mirrored. For our purposes the simple technique of outlining a pattern on a mirror (one that you buy or already have) and painting it is satisfactory. Draw the pattern on paper; cut out the paper, place it on a mirror, hold it down with a few pieces of Scotch tape, and outline the pattern in grease pencil. Remove the pattern and draw an outline in a suitable color. Fill in the outline (in the same way as for painting on glass)—the picture is completed. You can then put the mirror on a wall either without protection or with a thin piece of glass over it, held in place with a frame.

Another method of mirror painting is to tape the design on the mirror with masking tape. Do the design on paper as explained above and use masking tape to cover the part of mirror left exposed outside the pattern. This ensures clean, sharp lines. Once the painting is dry, remove the masking tape.

For mirror painting you will want to use enamels, because they are opaque and offer the best contrast to the silver surface. Transparent stains do not work effectively. Oil paints can be used but are somewhat more difficult to work with than enamels.

44. Painting a mirror with a fern design.

45. A commercially painted mirror.

PATTERNS

A simple pattern is best for a silhouette effect in one color—dark blue is handsome on silver, as is bright yellow. Too many colors on a mirror tend to defeat the decorative effect and can be too confusing, since silver is a vibrant color in itself.

A border pattern is highly effective because it frames the mirror; perhaps a small flower motif in one corner will give just the effect you want. A simple geometric border design also works well, but, no matter which design you select, the precision of the painting line creates the ultimate effect. Jagged lines look sloppy. Mirror painting is very much like silhouettes: the outline is paramount.

COLORED GLASS ON MIRRORS

Using colored glass on mirrors offers a unique way of creating a handsome picture. Small square or rectangular pieces of colored glass are used to create a total scene (but in this case you do not want a border effect). The fragmented pieces are glued to the mirror surface. You are using the mirror as a reflective background for a separate "painting." Experienced artists can create stunning designs with the colored-glass-on-mirror process and it is fun to do, although it requires infinite patience and care.

Make the pattern and number every piece of glass; keep a master pattern. Trace the pattern on the mirror in grease pencil and adhere the pieces with epoxy. If this is too much trouble, just sketch a pattern and set pieces in place randomly. The effect may not be as precise, but it will still be handsome.

MIRRORS

You can buy a mirror or use whatever you have on hand. For mirror painting inexpensive mirrors, called shock mirrors, are fine. These mirrors are ⅛-inch thick and have slight defects, but, once such a mirror is on a wall, the thickness will not be distinguishable and the slight defects will not be objectionable.

For your first attempts use the small hand mirrors that are sold at places such as Woolworths. They are inexpensive and good to practice on. For larger pictures use 8"-×-10" or 16"-×-20" mirrors, also sold in various stores, sometimes with frames. There are innumerable places to buy mirrors, but check around, because prices vary radically.

You cut mirror glass the same way as you do clear glass with one exception: the cut is made on the silvered side, and suitable edgework, such as grinding, seaming, or running Carborundum paper over rough edges, must be done before you start painting, or you might cut yourself.

9. Patterns

There are innumerable sources of patterns for glass painting—what you choose depends on your own personal taste. You can trace patterns from magazines or newspapers, make your own patterns, or, to get started, use a pattern from this book. Several different types of patterns are given here to help you get started.

To trace a pattern from this book, use a piece of carbon paper and a white sheet of paper. Put the carbon paper under the pattern and over the paper. Trace the outline, and you have a pattern. The sizes of the pattern may be changed by tracing it on grid paper (available at art stores) and copying it onto another piece of larger or smaller grid paper.

Most of the patterns that follow lend themselves well to transparent paints; some are best painted with acrylics. The pattern itself dictates the preferred type of paint, and, again, personal taste will influence the final selection. I have not prescribed certain paints for certain patterns: experiment and have some fun. I may like dark colors and you may like bright ones, but the important thing is to get you started painting on glass.

Once you have finished one or two pictures, you will want to do more. As mentioned earlier, there is a great fascination in painting on glass.

(continued on following page)

(continued from preceding page)

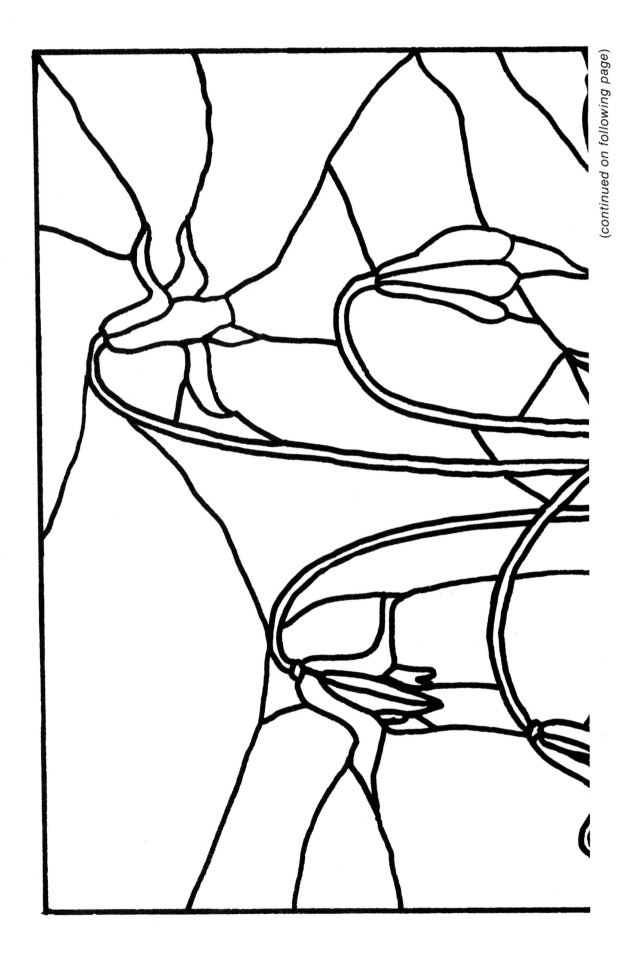

(continued on following page)

(continued from preceding page)

(continued on following page)

(continued from preceding page)

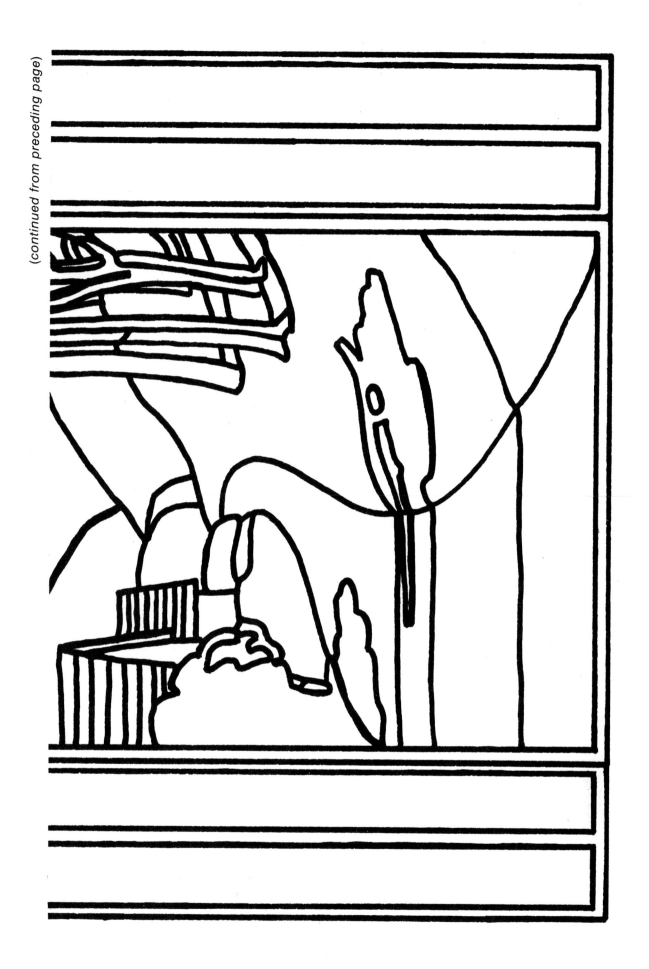

(continued on following page)

(continued from preceding page)

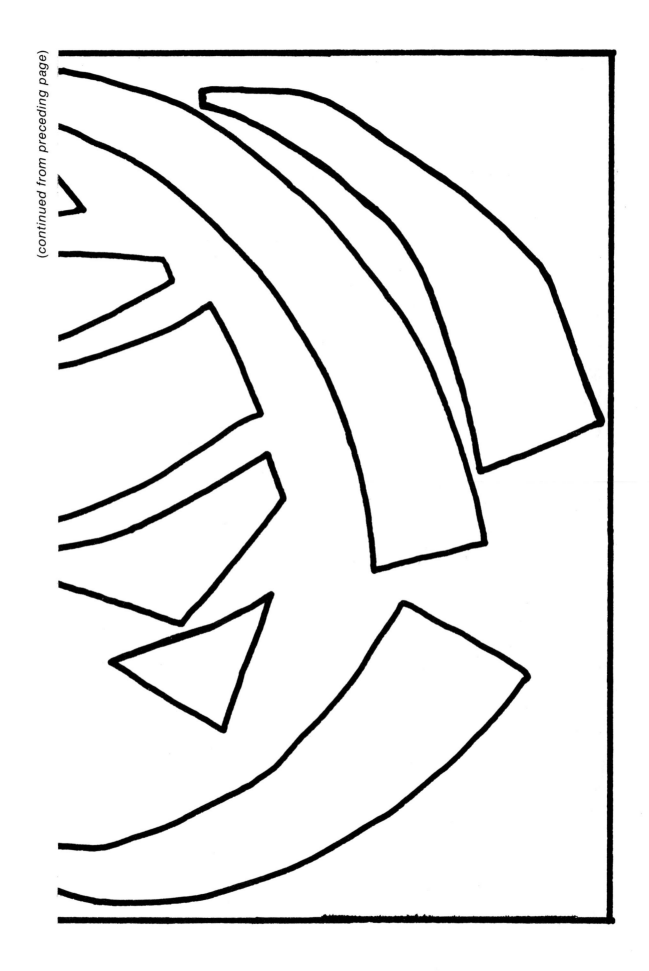

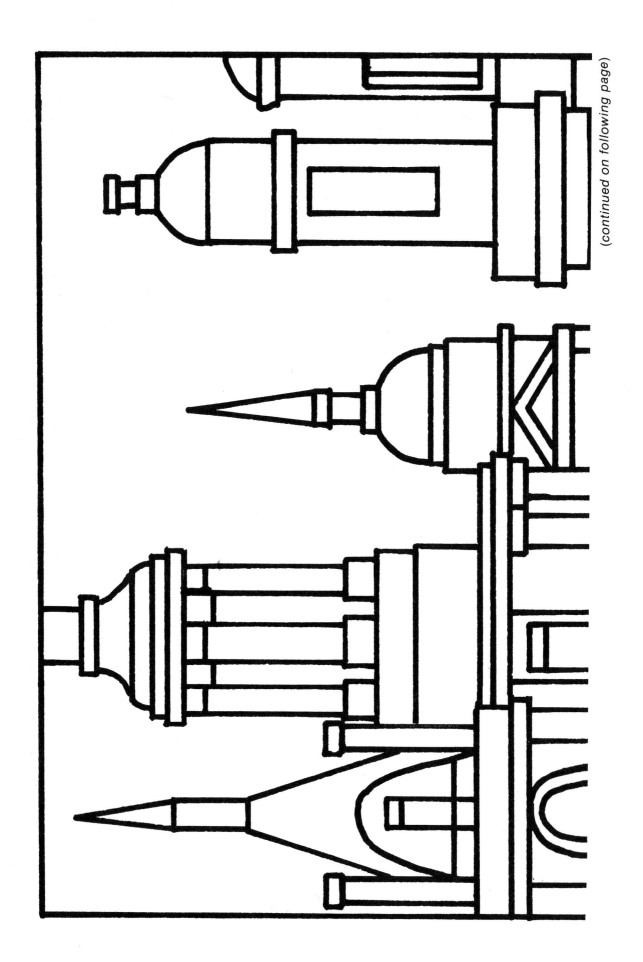

(continued on following page)

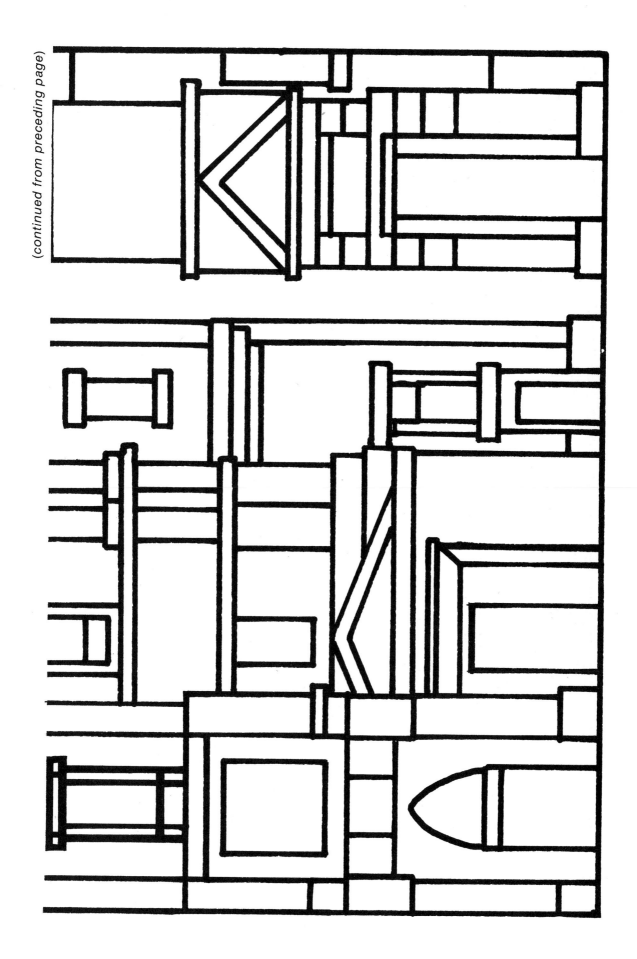

(continued from preceding page)

Where To Buy Supplies

Glues and epoxies for glass are sold at hardware stores and art shops. Read all labels carefully and be sure that the product you select will work on glass.

Paints are available in a variety of stores: art shops, craft shops, and some hardware stores. If you are searching specifically for transparent stains, call the art shop and ask for transparent paints that can be used on glass.

Glass is found at glass shops in your area. Check the Yellow Pages for your closest dealer. Most glass shops have both clear and colored glass. Many craft shops now carry a range of flat glass.

Index